Tiny Houses

The ultimate guide to tiny houses, shipping container homes, and building your own tiny house!

Table of Contents

Introduction

Thank you for taking the time to pick up this book about Tiny Houses!

This book covers the topic of Tiny Houses and sustainable living, and will teach you how you can begin to build your very own tiny home!

You will soon discover all about the Tiny House movement, and how thousands of others are adopting this more minimalistic and sustainable way of living. Tiny Houses are an excellent way to not only save money, but also to create a true architectural masterpiece, that may even (depending on your chosen design) be totally mobile!

At the completion of this book you will have a good understanding of Tiny Houses, and know what steps to take next to begin the building process of your very own. This includes knowledge of the entire building process, what considerations you'll need to make, and the legal side of building your own Tiny House!

Once again, thanks for taking the time to read this book, I hope you find it to be helpful!

Chapter 1:
What Are Tiny Houses?

Although Tiny Houses are constantly growing in popularity, there is still some dispute as to how exactly to define a Tiny House. Ultimately, advocates are usually most interested in how to best facilitate the satisfying lifestyle changes that occur due to serious downsizing.

How Small is Tiny?

There has been a lot of hype lately surrounding the idea of Tiny Houses. You may be asking yourself what all the fuss is about, or even on a more basic level: what exactly is a Tiny House to begin with?

As the name implies, Tiny Houses are much smaller than their more conventional counterparts. The definition of "tiny," however, is somewhat subjective. Most people consider "tiny" to describe any home that is 500 square feet or less in size, although even this definition leaves much room for personal interpretation. Some tiny houses are permanently affixed to foundations, while others are built on wheels with the intent of transporting them to their final destination.

Many in the Tiny House community choose to build their own homes using floor plans available online or even designing their own. Others hire contractors. Some Tiny Houses do not even resemble conventional houses at all. Those living in RVs and motor homes are often welcomed into Tiny House communities with open arms, as are more unconventional solutions such as shipping containers (we will cover this later), and converted sheds. Generally speaking, the term 'Tiny

House' is simply a term used to define any living space that is extremely small.

Of course each individual, couple, or family's space needs are different and must be considered when making the decision to adopt a Tiny House lifestyle. In addition to personal needs, the building codes regarding minimum square foot regulations for domiciles vary from place to place, which can impact design considerations. You can find both design tips and information about permits and how to meet local building codes in later chapters.

What's all the Fuss About?

Moving into a Tiny House often involves significant lifestyle changes, many of which can bring positive benefits into the lives of those who are willing to make them. Below are just a few of the many changes you can look forward to if you choose to make the switch to living small.

- **Save money.** Tiny Houses can be built quite inexpensively, particularly by those who are willing to put in some of the work themselves. But that's just the start of the savings. Conventional houses often come with extremely high monthly bills. The amount of heat, electricity, and water required to keep a household clean and provide for the needs of even a small family can be overwhelming. Look forward to much lower bills once you've made the move into your new Tiny House.

- **Encourage minimalism.** Many people have been choosing to push back against the rampant materialism that has overtaken our culture by embracing a minimalist lifestyle. Living in a Tiny House epitomizes this choice. Not only will you decrease your reliance on money by owning your own home instead of renting and lowering your monthly bills, you'll also decrease your reliance on needless belongings. With limited space, you can rest assured that you'll only want to have as much as you need to live a satisfying and de-cluttered life.

- **Go Off Grid.** Some Tiny House owners choose to tie into conventional electricity grids, but it is often unnecessary. Because the power needs of these revolutionary homes are so small, it is much more feasible to provide for them via alternative means such as solar panels or wind power.

- **Increased Portability.** How does the idea of having the freedom to pick up and move, but bring your home with you sound? By making the right design choices during the building process you can bring the comfort of home with you when you move, because you can just go ahead and bring your whole home along!

- **Design Versatility.** Those who choose to design and build their own Tiny Houses have much more control over what features they want to include and how they want their houses to be configured. You'll be surprised by how much working within the context of a smaller space can get those creative juices flowing and encourage innovative design features.

- **Spend Less Time Cleaning.** A smaller space means that you'll have less to worry about. In addition to accumulating less stuff, you'll have an easier time keeping what you do have clean and tidy!

- **Reduce Your Ecological Footprint.** Many proponents of Tiny House living have come to their conclusions at least partially based on the fact that it is a much more environmentally friendly way to live. You'll use up less resources both in constructing your home and in keeping it running, and an added benefit to Tiny House living is that you'll have more time to appreciate the natural world that you are helping to save, thanks to the money that *you'll* be saving.

Of course, these are only a few of the potential benefits reported by converts to Tiny House living. Others will be discussed in more detail later in this book, while yet more can only be discovered after making the move. It can be scary making the personal changes necessary to downsize successfully, but keeping some of these long term benefits in mind will make the whole process easier.

What Are the Common Challenges of Tiny House Living?

Any lifestyle change comes with its own set of sacrifices that need to be made and challenges that need to be met, and adopting a Tiny House lifestyle is not the exception to this rule. Below are a few of the challenges that people commonly report when making the switch, and also some solutions.

- **Lack of Privacy.** Particularly when it comes to Tiny House living with a family it can be hard sharing space to the degree that it will quickly become necessary. It can feel a little crowded in there. One solution? Use it as an excuse to spend more time outside the house. Everyone has interests and passions that they've been putting on the back burner to focus on making money to provide for their material needs. With these needs lessened, make use of new found time to go for walks, enjoy nature, or focus on personal goals outside the home. Alternatively, many families choose to build their Tiny Houses in the context of a dedicated community that has additional communal space set aside to allow individuals to focus on their houses as private space.

- **Accommodating Visitors.** If you frequently entertain guests from out of town, Tiny House living may pose some problems. Guests that are comfortable sharing their space and crashing on the couch for a few days will likely pose no problems. For those that require a little bit more personal space, here's one simple solution: consider purchasing a high quality tent!

- **Cooking Large Meals**. Cooking for the family should pose no problems even with limited kitchen space, but your Tiny House will not likely have the storage space for keeping large and infrequently used dishes necessary for cooking for large groups. This problem can also be solved by seeking out a community willing to devote extra space to communal kitchens in external buildings.

- **Less Storage Space**. It can be hard to make the transition from a large home into a Tiny House, as most of us acquire many possessions that we do not actually need over the course of our lives. If sorting through endless possessions all at once is posing too much of a problem, consider renting a storage unit. It's not a great long term solution, but it can buy you some extra time to ease into your new lifestyle.

Most people who make the change find that these and other potential issues can also be considered opportunities to challenge themselves and make positive changes in their lives. Those who simply can't bear the thought of parting with a 300-piece shoe collection may find these challenges insurmountable, but for anyone willing to sacrifice some material belongings and personal space, the benefits will likely outweigh them.

Chapter 2:
What Are Shipping Container Houses?

Shipping Container Houses represent one unique variety of alternative Tiny House construction that has been gaining popularity in recent years. These re-purposed homes start out their lives as cargo containers used to transport goods by boat or by rail. Like other Tiny Houses, they can be personalized endlessly to provide for any individual or family's needs. They do, however, come with some additional benefits and disadvantages that are not shared with other Tiny House models, which will be discussed below.

Why Choose a Shipping Container House?

- **They're Inexpensive.** Shipping container houses are usually at least 20% less expensive to build than comparably sized homes built out of more conventional materials. Used shipping containers are easily available all over the world and are designed specifically to be easily transported as well.

- **They Use Recycled Materials.** All Tiny Houses are more environmentally friendly than larger domiciles. Shipping Container Houses epitomize the ecological benefits of Tiny House living. They are made from recycled materials that would otherwise go unused, and do not require new trees to be cut for lumber.

- **They're Weather Resistant.** Shipping containers are designed to protect merchant's goods from storms at sea and a wide variety of environmental factors. They're both hurricane and fire proof as cargo containers before they become houses, which takes care of at least a few safety considerations.

So What's the Down Side?

- **Poor Response to Extreme Temperatures.** If you live in an area of the country that experiences extreme summer heat or winter cold, a Shipping Container House might not be for you. They can be insulated to better withstand temperature change, but most find that it isn't worth the extra expense and hassle.

- **Lack of Precedent.** There simply aren't a lot of Shipping Container Houses out there, which can pose unique challenges. It can be hard to find a contractor who knows how to work with the given materials, and furthermore it can be a nightmare trying to navigate complicated building codes that often do not have specific regulations concerning these obscure buildings.

Some people find that the local weather or building codes preclude the construction of Shipping Container Houses in their areas. Others are willing to go through the extra hassle of finding a suitable building site and feel that it is well worth it to live in a unique and environmentally conscious home that reflects their personality and values. Ultimately the choice is up to you!

Chapter 3:
What is the Tiny House Movement?

The Tiny House Movement is an architectural movement toward building smaller structures, but it is also a social movement that advocates for living more simply. In the United States the movement has grown in response to a drastic increase in the size of average family homes. As a movement, it strives to devalue showy displays of material wealth and instead place an emphasis back on healthier social wealth factors like connection with family and community.

A Little History

One of the earliest known Tiny House advocates was born far earlier than the movement itself: Henry David Thoreau wrote his famous work *Walden* while living in a structure just large enough to meet his material needs. He is often cited as an early inspiration for the movement.

The economic crisis that occurred in 2007 and 2008 attracted many more Tiny House and minimalism enthusiasts to the movement, as people began to recognize the benefits of living more simply and affordably.

Today Tiny Houses are receiving more media attention all the time. With real estate markets in many places precluding the possibility of buying a conventional home for even most fairly well off families, Tiny Houses provide a more affordable alternative.

Tiny House Communities

Many of those who choose to adopt a Tiny House lifestyle find that it is easier to do so in the context of a community of people who espouse similar values. These intentional communities often feature shared cooking or recreational spaces in addition to privately owned Tiny Homes, and can help to mitigate some of the challenges that living in such a small space can pose, particularly for those with families.

Some cities are adopting the idea of Tiny House communities as a solution to combat homelessness. Eugene, OR and Olympia, WA are just two examples of cities that have used revolutionary Tiny House ideals and technologies to create transitional living communities that can give homeless people a place to get on their feet and return toward participating as self-sufficient members of society.

Other communities are established by groups of like minded friends, or existing neighbors who have all grown equally weary of the monetary and social burdens of conventional living.

Online Tiny House Communities

Do you love the idea of building and living in your own Tiny House but hate the idea of doing it in the context of a larger community? Many Tiny House owners opt for a more autonomous approach, so you're not alone. However, even if you don't like the idea of intentional community infiltrating your real life, it can be helpful to become involved in online Tiny House communities in order to learn some of the tips and tricks you'll need to know to get around building codes, find land to build on, and make the most out of your space.

Start by checking out some of the many websites and forums that are already out there such as www.thetinylife.com or www.tinyhousecommunity.com. You've already gotten a good head start by reading this book, but an online forum or other community will offer you the opportunity to ask questions directly to those with experience as your project progresses and to share your personal experience with others.

It's a good idea to check out some pictures and posts before you get started constructing your own Tiny House. You'll find even more tips and tricks for dealing with different climate zones as well as beautiful pictures that will inspire you to think ahead to your own finished project!

Chapter 4:
How Much Will It Cost
to Build My Own?

There is no simple answer to the question of cost. Someone with construction experience can design and build a simple Tiny House for around $10,000 with new materials. On average those who opt for a do it yourself approach spend between $15,000 and $25,000. One man in Oakland specializes in building Tiny Houses out of reclaimed materials and averages $40/house! Ultimately the price tag attached to your new home will depend largely on how much of the labor you are willing to put in yourself, how complicated the design is, and how inventive you are in regards to building materials.

Typically, purchasing a prefabricated Tiny Home or paying a professional builder to construct one will cost between $30,000 and $50,000, again depending on the size and complexity of the design. For those looking to move in as soon as possible without the hassle of building their own houses but still want the design benefits of customized housing, the website www.tinyhousemap.com provides a listing of professional Tiny House builders all around the world. Prefabricated houses built by professionals and owners alike can be found online as well at www.tinyhouselistings.com. The price of purchasing a prefabricated house is generally lower than that of hiring someone to design and build a custom model, but it is still more expensive than taking on some of the work yourself.

Tips to Save Money Building Your Own Tiny House

- **Buy used whenever possible.** The Habitat Restore and website www.craigslist.org are both good places to find cheap construction materials. Just be sure that everything you buy is in good condition.

- **Consider alternative building materials.** Function, not fashion, is the priority of most Tiny House builders and owners. Try not to feel wedded to any particular building material until you have evaluated all the pro's and con's as well as taken a look at the associated price tag. Some notable exceptions: spend the extra money on adequate insulation and decent quality windows. You'll save it in the long run in heating and cooling costs.

- **Purchase cheaper appliances.** You'll probably require smaller appliances to match your new smaller home, but that doesn't mean you have to go all out and buy name brand everything. Do your research before purchasing anything new or used to ensure that your appliances will withstand the test of time, but try not to get sucked in by flashy gimmicks like refrigerators with televisions built into the door. Remember: that's the kind of materialism that your new lifestyle strives to avoid. Another great tip: old RVs are a treasure trove of space saving appliances that you can get for extremely cheap or sometimes for free.

- **Do the Labor Yourself**. Or enlist your friends to help you. Make them dinner or work trade with them, helping them with some other task that requires an extra set of hands. The labor accounts for the majority of the cost of having a Tiny House built professionally, and most of it can be done quickly and efficiently by just a few people with a little bit of construction experience.

Chapter 5:
Where Do I Get Started?

First decide whether you would prefer to build your own home or pay someone else to do it for you. The approach that you choose will determine your next steps and how large of a role you will play in the design and construction phases ahead.

Tips for Taking a DIY Approach

If you find the idea of designing and building your own Tiny House exciting rather than intimidating, this section is for you! However, there is no shame in hiring a professional to do the work for you if you aren't sure if your carpentry skills are up to par. Also keep in mind that you can do as much of the work as possible yourself and contract out skilled labor to someone who can perform the rest of it safely.

In the next chapters you will find more in-depth information about each step in the design and building process, but first let's take a look at some basic considerations to keep in mind throughout the process.

- **Know Your Needs.** If you love to spend your time cooking for your family, keep in mind during the design process that this will mean you'll probably need to devote a little bit more space to the kitchen area. Do you share a bed with someone? If so, be sure to allocate enough space. There are plenty of solutions for hideaway beds and building extra storage into your design to compensate for the space required for these types of needs, but we'll talk about that later.

- **Prioritize Open Space.** A Tiny House can easily feel cramped if proper consideration is not given to including as much open space as possible. This means avoiding unnecessary partitions and walls, and using rooms for as many different purposes as possible. Carefully placed windows and mirrors and choosing light colored paints later in the process can also go a long way toward helping to alleviate potential claustrophobia.

- **Location and Direction.** By choosing the right location and placing windows correctly, you can drastically improve your Tiny House's passive solar heating and cooling capacity, make the best possible use of natural sunlight in your home, and cut down even further on energy bills. You will need to have a location in mind to make use of these techniques. At the very least take note of the latitude and climate region of any area you are considering for a permanent or semi-permanent building site, as these will help you determine where to place your windows for maximum effect.

- **Take Some Notes Along the Way.** Be sure to write down any questions or conclusions that you come up with along the way as you begin to give some thought to what has inspired you to make the move to Tiny House living and how that will be reflected in your new living space.

Now that you've got a few basic considerations to keep in mind throughout the process, it's time to get started for real. The next chapter focuses on the initial design phase and includes resources for sample floor plans to look at for inspiration. The following chapters discuss what you'll need to complete your project, followed by a discussion of legal considerations. Don't get too ahead of yourself; you'll probably want to read through them all before you break out the hammer and nails.

Chapter 6:
Tiny House Design

Whether you are intending on doing most of the work yourself or are working with a professional Tiny House designer or builder, there are a few things that you can do to ensure that the final product will live up to your expectations. Some people love to express themselves and become directly involved in every aspect of the design process, while others prefer a completely hands off approach.

Those with sufficient construction experience who are more focused on getting started and getting it done than considering all the particulars might want to consider purchasing pre-made plans and just jumping right in. Note that there are plenty of Tiny House plans available, but they're not all created equal. Shop around before making a final decision and purchase if this is the route you decide to take.

What to Expect if You Purchase Designs

If you decide to buy existing Tiny House designs, be sure that they include the following items. If you're starting from scratch, keep in mind that these documents are included in purchased plans for a reason, and try to replicate them for yourself!

- **A Cover Sheet.** This is an artists rendering of what your house will look like from the outside when it is finished. If you're designing your own plan, think of this as the inspiration phase rather than an exact replica.

- **Floor Plan.** A floor plan or layout will show the dimensions of each room, including door and window locations and where to place plumbing fixtures. Find some additional tips on creating your own accurate floor plans below.

- **Foundation Plan.** This plan will only be included if the design is for a stationary home rather than a Tiny House on wheels. It will include dimensions for concrete walls and footings as well as information about retaining walls.

- **Structural Plan.** A structural plan should include the details necessary to complete the ceiling and loft if present as well as the roof and the frame.

- **Roof Plan.** Information such as the intended materials and angles of slopes as well as dimensions and locations of chimneys and any decorative elements should be available in a roof plan.

- **Wall Section.** Not all purchased building plans will come with a wall section or cross section, but they can be helpful. They show a side view of rooms in the home that can elucidate changes in height and specify details about what materials to use.

- **Electrical Plan.** This drawing should show the intended locations for any fixtures, outlets, and switches.

You should not necessarily expect all of these elements to be present in free plans that you find online, but if you're going to purchase professional design plans you may as well try to get what you can for the money you are putting in.

Get Some Inspiration From Existing Designs

Many owners and designers of existing Tiny Houses are enthusiastic about sharing their experiences with others looking to follow in their footsteps. It can be extremely helpful to take advantage of this! Check out sites like www.tinyhousedesign.com and other websites and forums to see what other people have done. Existing designs can be a great place to start, and observing what other people have done to make the best use of space can be a source of inspiration for you while you design your own home.

You don't need to just pick an existing design plan and stick with that, although if someone's design really resonates with you there is no reason not to. Take the ideas that you like and try to find ways to incorporate them into your own Tiny House design!

Put it Down on Paper

Do a few quick sketches to get down some ideas for what you want. Keep in mind the conclusions you came to in your earlier brainstorming sessions about how you want space to be designated and how you are going to meet you or your family's basic needs. You don't need to be an artistic genius to do this; it's not intended to directly reproduce exactly what you want, but instead to give a basic idea of where things go and how they relate to one another.

The next set of drawings will be more helpful if they are drawn to scale. This will help you understand how much space you have to work with and how big each element you want to include really is in comparison to all of the other elements. Using graph paper and assigning consistent size values to each square will be extremely helpful here.

Some people find it helpful to use architectural drawing software to help in the initial design phases. There's no need to drop half your yearly salary on a professional program like Auto CAD. Many web based design tools are available online for free. One example popular among Tiny House designers is SketchUp, available for your use at www.sketchup.com. If you don't love it, that's okay! There are many other programs available, and comparable results can be produced with a pencil, paper, and a little extra time.

Take Size Seriously

Knowing exactly how much space each element that will be included in your design is going to take up is extremely important. This is particularly true for those of you planning to build on a trailer. Ideally the weight of your home with all of its permanent fixtures already installed should be under 10,000 lbs. In addition, keep in mind that most states require that the load on a trailer be no more than 8'6" wide and 13'6" high to move them without having to get special permits or licenses.

Whether you plan on going mobile or building on a foundation, don't forget things like walls, doors, and windows. Know how thick the walls are going to be, or at least make a good educated guess. It's also likely that your doors and windows will not be the same size as those in conventional houses. Try to be realistic about how much space will be required for doors and windows and include these measurements in your design. This should include the amount of space that it will take to swing the door open.

When it comes to furniture, you'll likely want to go light on it. Quite frankly unused furniture just takes up too much space. Anything that you do not need or use on an almost daily basis does not belong in your new home.

Understanding size and dimensions can be particularly challenging when it comes to the kitchen. Typical kitchen cabinets are between one and two feet deep, and counters require even more space. Most people find that between 36 and 48 inches of counter space that is dedicated specifically to cooking work is a comfortable amount. Other tables and flat surfaces can often be folded or raised to provide more space. In the kitchen this is less true because you'll need that cabinet space for storage. Be sure to include enough space in your design to accommodate your cooking needs.

Bathroom Design Concerns

If you're looking for ways that you can fit an entire bathroom into a very small amount of space, just take a look at a fully equipped RV. Be sure to leave enough space around your toilet for comfortable use. You'll also want to get used to the idea of a standing shower, as most people will not want to devote the amount of space necessary for a full bath tub.

Keep in mind that you'll need to make accommodations in your design for necessary plumbing. This is also true of the kitchen. Bathroom walls will likely need to be thicker, and if you plan on taking your Tiny House off the grid you'll need to account for water storage tanks as well.

One way of avoiding the hassle of a black water tank or other permanent sewage system is considering a composting toilet. Modern models take up only a small amount of space, do not require external plumbing, and often avoid the need for electricity as well. If you're thinking to yourself "ew, what about the smell?" then you haven't done enough research yet.

True DIY enthusiasts interested in composting toilets will want to check out Joseph Jenkins' *The Humanure Handbook*. Building your own composting toilet will ensure that it meets all of your household's needs and almost completely eliminate the associated costs. A DIY humanure toilet can be built for next to nothing using primarily materials that you will likely already have. It would, however, require an entire book to devote enough space and time to discussing the practical concerns of health and safety, so give the handbook a read before attempting this project for yourself.

Raising the Roof

Choosing the right roof is about more than aesthetics. First and foremost, your roof serves as a primary defense against the elements. This means that if your home is built on a foundation you should primarily consider the climate of the area you've chosen to call home when choosing what style to use. If you plan to build your Tiny Home on a trailer and take it on the road, take that into consideration as well. Below are a few common choices that embrace both function and fashion.

- **Shed Roof.** Most sheds use a one side roof, which in the context of Tiny House living allows a little bit of extra space for a loft should you choose to incorporate this feature. The ability to include extra windows is another plus, as it will allow for better use of passive lighting. For those planning on going off grid, a one sided shed roof will also make rainwater collection much easier, as it will all drain to the same side. However, this style's main disadvantage is a serious concern for those living in colder climates: if the area you plan on living in gets a lot of snow, you'll have to compensate by increasing the roof's pitch to avoid structural damage. No matter where you live you'll also want to keep in mind that the peak of the roof will represent the maximum height of your structure. The most commonly used material for this type of roof is metal, which has the added benefit of keeping snow accumulation to a minimum in comparison to other materials.

- **Saltbox Roof.** This option has the added space benefit of the shed roof described above but comes to a peak off center. This advantage is one of its few up sides. Most Tiny House owners avoid this style of roofing because its off center peak requires extra fortification in the eaves. It also places added limitations on where you can place doors and windows due to structural concerns: they must be placed on the longer side of the structure rather than on its side.

- **Gable Roof.** A Gable roof is traditionally the most common roofing style among both normally sized houses and their Tiny counterparts. It's simple to construct, with just one centrally placed peak, and can utilize a wider variety of roofing materials successfully. If you choose a Gable roof you'll be sacrificing some space for the sake of convenience, though. In areas that receive heavy snowfall you'll have to reinforce it properly, which will take about 12 inches of additional space.

- **Gambrel Roof.** Most commonly identified with barns, this center peaked roofing style lends some extra space and is more structurally sound than simple gable roofs. Its construction is more complicated than other styles, but many Tiny House builders find that the extra space and structural integrity make the extra work well worth the effort.

- **Flat Roof.** Although popular in some desert areas, flat roofs are simply not practical for most climates. They accumulate water, snow, and debris much more easily, requiring more frequent maintenance and repair. Unless you live in an area that receives next to no rain or you're willing to devote significant energy to roof maintenance, the ease of installation is not worth the hassle you'll be trading for later on down the line.

- **Arched Roof.** A rounded roof, if properly constructed, will be extremely structurally sound. This is because an arch can disperse the load more evenly across its surface than even a Gambrel roof. However, they are easily the most challenging and expensive roofs to build so this option is not for everyone.

A Note About Skylights

Although skylights can add a certain visual appeal to a home, allowing in more natural light, don't be fooled: they will make your home less energy efficient rather than more. When the sun is at its highest and you require shade it will be shining directly through your skylight. In the cold winter months when the sun is closer to the horizon you'll be left with a useless window in your roof that lets out all of the warm air and does little in the way of allowing in more ambient light. Simply put, there are better ways to make a visual statement.

Designing for Climate

If you plan on putting down roots in a cold area, be sure to keep the weather in mind when making important design choices. In addition to choosing a roof style that can accommodate large amounts of weight from snowfall you'll also want to include heavier insulation. Insulate the walls, floor, and roof with rigid foam and consider adding spray foam to further increase the R-value of your insulation.

Buy a heating system that is appropriate to the local climate and accommodate for it in your initial design phase. A wood heater, propane heater, or even an electric heater will all do, but be sure that you allow space in your plans for any associated pipes and vents. For areas that tend toward high humidity in colder months it should be noted that a wood stove can double as a dehumidifier.

It's worth spending the extra money on double or even triple pane windows if you live someplace extremely cold. You'll make up the difference in the long run on heating costs and will avoid a whole lot of hassle.

Designing for Self-Sufficiency

One of the many things that makes Tiny Houses so popular is their limited resource use. It doesn't take anywhere near as much electricity to light one or a few small rooms as it does an entire house. You can reduce your electrical consumption even further by purchasing hand tools instead of their electric counterparts and reducing your reliance on electrical kitchen appliances. After all, people got along just fine for centuries before the relatively recent advent of electricity.

Many people who opt for adopting a more traditional lifestyle in which they put in the little bit of extra manual labor that is necessary to, say, mix together the ingredients for a cake by hand instead of owning a dedicated electrical cake mixer find that they take satisfaction from accomplishing these tasks by hand. Doing more things the old fashioned way, and owning less specialized equipment is also a great way to reduce clutter, which is essential when you are working with only a very small amount of space.

If your energy needs are sufficiently low, it will come with another added benefit: you'll be more likely to be able to provide for them by generating your own power instead of hooking in to a power grid. Roof top solar panels have become remarkably energy efficient and inexpensive in recent years, and can be used to provide at least the majority of your power if not all of it, assuming you're willing to fully embrace a more minimalist lifestyle in conjunction with your minimalist living space.

Those who do plan on installing solar panels should take this into account from the beginning if at all possible, as it will help to determine how electrical wiring will be laid and what exactly will be necessary. Whether you plan to go solar or not, you can save yourself a lot of hassle later down the line by placing light fixtures and electrical outlets in sensible places that are both easy to get to once the house is finished and easy to wire in the process.

Consider whether or not your home will be connected to a traditional water and sewage system as well. If you plan on hooking into town water, it will require different plumbing accommodations than providing your own water. Many of those who choose to build their own Tiny Houses opt for taking shower fixtures from existing RVs. This is an inexpensive option that comes complete with all of the necessary water tanks.

Providing your own water and power will both increase your home's self-sufficiency and make it easier to move your Tiny House should you decide to do so.

Taking the Show on the Road

Many Tiny House dwellers cite the portability of their new homes as one of their primary sources of appeal. You can take full advantage of this by building your Tiny House directly onto an existing trailer.

Designing your Tiny House to be fully mobile also increases your choices when it comes to finding the perfect location. It opens up possibilities such as taking up temporary residence in RV and trailer parks that would not allow renters to build permanent structures. Having a Tiny House that is officially classified as a trailer can also help get around restrictive building codes.

By designing your home to be as self-sufficient as possible you will also increase your ability to pick up and move with less hassle. A composting toilet, water holding tanks, and small solar panel array will allow you to set down wherever you please without having to worry about how you will provide for your basic household needs once you get there.

If you do plan on moving frequently, make sure to construct your external walls out of materials that will be able to hold up to strong winds and the associated vibration of traveling on a trailer at highway speeds. Also be sure to check with your local DMV regarding size and weight requirements for trailers.

Which Contractors Will I Need to Hire?

The answer to this question obviously depends on your level of expertise in the various areas of construction, plumbing, and electrical work as well as the specific design of your Tiny House. If you have any doubts as to your ability to complete these tasks on your own, there is no shame in enlisting some professional help, particularly when there are safety concerns at play.

Even if you have carpentry experience and plan on doing most of the work yourself, you should probably trust the electrical wiring to a professional. This can be dangerous work for someone who doesn't know what they are doing, and can pose long term risks down the road that could lead to fire hazards.

You will likely also want to hire a professional plumber to properly install pipes and vents, regardless of whether or not you plan on going off the grid eventually. The last thing you want is to build your dream home and have it flooded due to faulty plumbing. This is particularly important for those who intend to hook into municipal water supplies.

The Tiny House movement is completely in favor of adopting a DIY attitude, but there is a limit. A good rule of thumb is: if doing it wrong could lead to fire, flood, or other potential disaster it's best to spend the extra money and trust the work to a professional.

Even if you feel completely confident in performing all of these tasks yourself, if you're not a professional contractor you should try to have all of your design plans evaluated by someone with experience.

Chapter 7:
What Will I Need to
Build My Tiny House?

This chapter will take a look at the tools and experience necessary to complete the basic construction of your Tiny House. It should help you decide whether or not you plan to do this work yourself, and if you do it will tell you what will be required.

Tools and Gear

Having the right tools and safety gear will make all the difference in terms of the finished product. Depending on your specific design considerations you may need additional tools, but this list covers everything required to get started on a basic design. Most of them are tools that the majority of home owners have on hand anyhow, but consider purchasing everything you need before you get started to save time later if there are items on the list that you do not have.

If your design does not use a metal roof, keep that in mind and don't bother purchasing things like angle grinders and power shears. The descriptions of each tool below indicate what area of the project they will be most useful for; use that as a guide when purchasing tools.

Hand Tools

- **Hammer.** Some of the work you'll need to do can be done with either a nail gun or an impact driver, but you should still have a sturdy hammer on hand. If you're starting from the ground up in purchasing tools, this is a good excuse to buy a high quality hammer. Putting in the extra money on a name brand that comes with a warranty is worth the small difference in price as you'll surely be using a hammer for more than just this one project.

- **Screwdrivers.** Every home owner should have a good and diverse set of screwdrivers. If you don't, look for a well made set made of good quality steel and select one that comes with various sizes. You'll likely need both flat head and Phillip's head screwdrivers to complete both this project and future work.

- **Lineman's Pliers.** This oddly named tool is actually quite simple in construction: it is a large, usually at least 9 inches long, set of combined pliers and wire cutters. The longer handles allow you to cut through thicker wiring in comparison to regular wire cutters. This is one tool where it's acceptable to look at the lower end less expensive varieties as a higher price tag on lineman's pliers doesn't necessarily correlate to higher quality.

- **Wire Strippers.** This multipurpose tool derives its name from its primary use in stripping the sheathing from wires. However, they can also be used in a pinch as wire cutters, screw cutters, and even pliers. This is another category where quality makes a big difference, particularly if you intend on doing your own electrical work. Using name brand wire strippers will make your life much easier, and particularly if the brand you choose is spring loaded it can speed up installation.

- **Utility Knife.** This incredibly useful tool will likely come in handy repeatedly over the course of both the design and construction phases of building your home. Choose either a folding knife or a more substantial full sized knife, but be sure that the blade is easy to remove and change.

- **Tin Snips.** These will primarily be used for cutting through metal sheeting. You will likely not need them until you get to installing the flashing and roof, but they may come in handy for other jobs as well. Consider buying a three pack in order to have access to different sizes.

- **PVC Cutter.** Although you can use other tools to do the same job, PVC cutters are inexpensive and provide a cleaner cut than, say, a miter saw.

- **Nail Puller.** It's entirely possible that you'll get through your project without needing a nail puller, but if you do end up making any framing mistakes you'll be glad to have it.

- **Flat Bar.** This is another periphery tool. You may not end up needing it, but a flat bar certainly comes in handy if you need to make small adjustments to doors or windows in order to get them exactly square. It will also make installing your flooring much easier. Look for a bar with a curved shaft, as this reduces flexing and increases rigidity. Particularly when you're building in a small space, it will make your life much easier.

Measuring Tools

We all know the old axiom, "measure twice, cut once." But your measurements will only be as accurate as the tools you use to take them. Having these on hand from the very beginning of your project will ensure that you won't be making costly mistakes.

- **Tape Measure.** Whether or not you have construction or handyman experience, your household is likely to already have a tape measure. Be sure that the one you're using is of high quality, as a cheap tape measure can provide no end of frustration to its user. 25 feet is the ideal length, as it will be long enough to take all of your measurements but will not be as bulky as its longer counterparts. Buy a tape measure that is thick enough to extend out as far as you need it to without collapsing under its own weight.

- **Carpenter's Pencil.** It may sound superfluous to someone without building experience, but carpenters have specially designed pencils for a reason. Their added thickness makes it possible to mark up rougher wood. A dozen pencils should last you throughout the entire construction process.

- **Chalk Line.** You'll need a chalk line for installing flooring and siding, as it will allow you to mark straight lines over extended lengths of material. Go for a brand that uses blue chalk over red, as the red is much harder to remove when you're done.

- **Level.** Levels are useful in ensuring that lumber is placed exactly parallel or perpendicular to the ground as needed. Levels fall under the category of absolutely necessary measurement devices, as without them all the pieces are unlikely to fit together correctly and the structural integrity of your house will suffer. Four feet is typically the best length, as it is short enough to fit in most spaces but long enough to ensure accuracy. You should test your level in the store before buying it.

- **Carpenter's Square.** This is primarily useful for building in rafters or stairs. It's essentially just a ruler that is constructed at a ninety-degree angle, allowing its user to measure distance in two directions from the same point. As such it's not absolutely essential, but it will save you a whole load of time and hassle for a minimal amount of money. If you do buy a carpenter's square, go for aluminum; it will hold up better to the test of time.

- **Speed Square.** This tool is used during the framing process. You will use it to mark locations for studs in top plates and kick plates, so make sure it is around seven inches long.

- **Plywood Square.** Also known as a drywall square, this tool is used to draw straight lines on plywood and drywall. Mark this under the category of convenient, but not essential; a chalk line can be used to the same end, the plywood square will just save you some time.

Power Tools

Some converts to the minimalist aspects of Tiny House living will argue against the use of power tools, but if you're not looking to invest huge amounts of time and physical labor just for the privilege of labeling yourself a purist it's strongly suggested that you purchase or rent them anyhow. The right power tools will shave many hours of work off your project time and save you much frustration and many blisters. Don't anticipate having the space to store them once you're done? You can rent these tools by the hour or the day at any Home Depot and many other hardware stores.

- **Drill and Drill Bits.** Along with an impact driver, a cordless power drill will be one of the most frequently used tools in your arsenal for this project. Given how likely it is that you will need them for other projects in the future, it's a good idea to spend the extra money and purchase a professional quality drill and drill bits. You will need different drill bits depending on the material you are working with, so go ahead and just buy the entire kit. Titanium bits cost a bit more than their cobalt and standard steel alternatives, but their drastically increased lifespan makes up for the initial investment cost.

- **Impact Driver and Driver Bits.** The same goes for impact drivers. This useful tool will likely come in handy in the future, so invest some extra money into one that will last. When looking at impact driver bits, take a moment to evaluate whether any kit you are considering actually covers the different bits that you will need as many do not have as much variety as will be required.

- **Hole Saw.** A hole saw is more or less a necessity for installing plumbing. You will use it to cut holes in both the floors and the walls through which your pipes will fit. Be sure to purchase a hole saw big enough to meet your needs. Look for 2 1/8 inch and 3 1/8 inch bits, and think about purchasing them individually instead of in a kit since these are most likely to be the sizes you will require for installing both exhaust vents and drain pipes.

- **Miter Saw.** This is easily the most important power tool to have. Just about every piece of wood that goes into your project, with the notable exception of that used for sheathing, can be cut with a miter saw. There is a vast difference between saws in different price ranges, so if you don't have it in the budget to purchase a high quality saw, consider renting.

- **Circular Saw.** As noted above a miter saw is not helpful in cutting sheathing. This is where the circular saw comes in. Find a saw that has a good balance between weight and power, as a heavier saw may pack some extra punch but will likely tire you out keeping it under control.

- **Table Saw.** A table saw performs many of the same functions as a circular saw, but removes some of the hassle. Instead of moving the saw, it remains stationary and you move the material to be cut beneath it. For those on a tight budget this tool is not absolutely necessary, but do consider purchasing a rip cut attachment for the circular saw you already own or rent. This will keep the saw blade at the right distance from the edge of whatever you are cutting.

- **Jigsaw.** This is definitely a tool that you should rent rather than buy unless you have specific future projects in mind that require its use. Jigsaws have the advantage over circular saws of being able to make curved cuts, which may come in handy for some home builders. Others will find that there is no need for a jigsaw. Evaluate your Tiny House design before deciding whether it's even worth renting this tool.

- **Angle Grinder.** An angle grinder can be a handy tool to have if you're constructing your roof from metal. Tin snips or electric shears can both serve a similar purpose, but they are much more difficult to maneuver. Although angle grinders are easier to use in these circumstances, they can be a bit unpredictable. You should be wearing safety gear throughout the construction process, but before using an angle grinder its important to take a moment to make sure you are.

- **Power Shears.** Power shears can run toward the expensive side, so you'll probably want to rent them rather than buy. They will be indispensable to you for perhaps several days if you are working with metal roofing.

- **Framing Nail Gun**. You'll only require this tool if you intend on nailing the framing together instead of screwing it. Using the nail gun has speed and ease of use as its primary benefits over using screws and a drill. With a framing nail gun, you could easily finish framing your entire Tiny House in a day.

A Few Words About Air Compressors

Air compressors are a great way to power your tools, and may be necessary depending on what power tools you've purchased. If your Tiny House is the only project that you anticipate needing an air compressor to complete, go for a less expensive pancake compressor. They don't produce enough power for, say, a professional contractor, but for your purposes they should work just fine and are much less expensive. You may also want to consider renting.

Last But Absolutely Not Least: Safety Gear

Don't be fooled by the placement of this section. Safety gear is an absolute must for any construction project, whether you're an amateur handyman or a DIY construction pro. As noted above you can get away with taking some of those tools off your must have list, but you cannot cut corners when it comes to safety gear. This cannot be emphasized enough.

- **Eye Protection**. It doesn't need to be fancy, but you do need to wear some form of safety glasses or goggles during all parts of the construction process. Those who wear prescription glasses may be tempted to skip this important safety feature, since it can be a little bit harder to find goggles and glasses that fit over them. Don't give in to this temptation. Regular glasses will not cut it; you need real gear.

- **Ear Protection**. If you're using power tools, you likely won't need to be told twice to use ear protection. Most people prefer over the head ear muffs to ear plugs, but this one is really left up to personal preference.

- **Gloves.** This is particularly important for working with metal roofing, as it can have sharp edges and be quite slippery.

- **Respirator.** You really only need to take this precaution when using paint or staining wood, or if you are working with PVC cement. Inhaling the noxious fumes that these chemicals produce is just not good for

anyone. Avoiding inhalation is worth the minor hassle
of buying and using a respirator when necessary.

43

Chapter 8:
Legal Concerns

Unfortunately, Tiny Houses currently exist in an ambiguous legal middle ground. However, even in counties that do not have specific accommodations in their laws there are often loopholes that Tiny House owners can exploit in order to get around minimum space requirements.

What About Building Codes?

Much of the hassle surrounding building codes can be avoided by finding a municipality that does not have restrictive building codes. Ask the following questions when you are deciding where to build and place your new Tiny House:

- Are there county or municipality minimum square foot requirements for residential dwellings that are built on foundations?

- Are there laws specifically allowing or disallowing the building of Tiny Houses in backyards of existing homes or on vacant properties? It can be helpful to put down your roots someplace where others have already laid the groundwork of obtaining legal exemptions for tiny living.

- Are there time limits or additional regulations about camping on private land? This is only relevant if you plan on building on a trailer.

The best place to find out what local building codes exist is to go to the Planning Department at the local City Hall. This office can only help you if you intend on building on a foundation. Those who prefer to build their Tiny Houses on trailers are instead subject to RV code requirements, which will be discussed below.

If you're shopping around for land over a larger area, you may not be able to physically walk into each individual Planning Department. As an alternative you can also look up the Residential Building Codes and local building requirements for each location you're investigating. These can typically be found on each city's official website under a Planning or Development department page.

The most common legal issue that stationary Tiny House dwellers face is minimum square foot requirements. Many areas stipulate minimum space requirements for any building intended as a primary residence. These requirements are sometimes less stringent when the structure is officially classified as an accessory dwelling, but this means that it must be constructed and permanently located on a property that also has a normal sized house.

What About That Trailer Thing?

Building your Tiny House on a trailer and having it officially classified as an RV can help you to get around minimum space requirements, but it is not a miracle cure to solve all of your legal problems. Some areas require RVs to be parked only in designated trailer or RV parks, which places some pretty severe limitations on where you will be able to live. Check to ensure that you can legally place a trailer for habitation on land before you buy it.

Another solution is to purchase land that is already zoned for multiple family living, such as apartment complexes or trailer parks. It is often already set up to legally accommodate small dwellings such as Tiny Homes, but you'll have to do some extra work to find a piece of land with the right zoning.

What Permits Will I Need?

If you're already uncomfortable with the idea of living in a legal middle zone, you'll definitely want to stay on top of permits. The best you can really do in terms of building and living legally in your new Tiny House is to put it on a trailer and register it appropriately at the DMV. The associated fees will likely be cheaper than building permits, but they will not universally cover all Tiny Houses in all localities so you're still only as legal as you can practically be. Head to the DMV and register it as a mobile home. It's really the closest you can come to being completely legal.

As more people become interested in Tiny Houses, laws in places that they are popular are beginning to change. If you have some extra time and money to devote to fighting the good fight, consider hiring a lawyer and collecting signatures to have the building codes changed to accommodate smaller dwelling spaces.

The first step toward doing so is to head to take a look at existing building codes and relevant laws. They are often obscure and a real challenge to learn, and this is the first time a lawyer would come in handy. Once you have a good grasp of what you're working with, head to the local Code Enforcement office and ask them what you need to do to obtain an exception.

You may have to speak with a specializing contractor, regardless of whether or not you have built your own Tiny House, who can act as an expert on the subject matter in the event that you need to provide evidence of your home's safety. Bring this contractor with you to your scheduled meeting with the Code Enforcement officer.

If you are comfortable with living in a legal gray zone and the possibility that you may eventually have to move, check out www.tinyhouseparking.com or www.tinyhousehosting.com for Tiny House friendly parking in your area.

Chapter 9:
Foundation Types

The first step in building your tiny house is often overlooked during the planning process – choosing the foundation type.

For mobile tiny homes, this will obviously not be necessary, but for those building standard tiny homes, or container homes, this step is extremely important!

The foundation type best suited to you will be dependent on a variety of factors. A few things you must consider when making your choice are: your structural needs, local government requirements, budget, and soil type.

During this phase of the planning process it would be wise to consult with a structural engineer as foundation requirements will vary on a case-by-case basis.

If you are building on a soft soil type, a deeper foundation will obviously be required. But do not simply guess this on your own – consult a professional to evaluate your particular needs.

Concrete Piers

Concrete piers are the first type of foundation that we will be looking at.

These are usually the most cost-effective type of foundation, and are relatively simple. Basically, they are concrete cubes that have steel bars inside of them to provide reinforcement.

Concrete piers can be made yourself inexpensively, and are also are cheap to acquire. They physically lift your house off of the ground, allowing for good ventilation, drainage, and protection against flooding.

Slab On Grade

A slab on grade is the next type of foundation we will be looking at.

For the extremely-small tiny houses, this will not likely be the foundation you choose. For tiny houses on the bigger end however, this foundation type could be perfect!

Slab on grade is a time-consuming and expensive foundation type, but it does have its benefits. Slab on grade is extremely stable and is suitable for all soil types.

This form of foundation might want to be avoided in colder climates however, as the slab can become quite cold, lowering the houses temperature further.

Pile Foundations

Pile foundations are the most expensive form of foundation, but in some circumstances are the only suitable choice. This type of foundation will be used when the soil is too weak to support a standard concrete slab.

Piles are cylindrical steel poles that are driven deep into the ground. They provide a very stable foundation, but due to the depth they need to be driven are quite expensive and time-consuming to use.

Once the piles are in place they are usually capped with additional concrete.

If you choose this type of foundation, it is recommended that you consult with a professional rather than trying to do it all yourself, as constructing piles can be a complicated process.

Chapter 10:
Portable Tiny Homes

Portable tiny homes are not only some of the coolest tiny houses around, they can often also be a lot cheaper to create in the first place!

If you use mostly second-hand materials, it's totally possible to create an awesome portable tiny house for less than $10,000! A fantastic place to find suitable 2nd hand materials is Craigslist. If you have a truck or a trailer that you can use to pick up the materials you find, that will make things a lot easier and cost-effective.

The first thing you will need to purchase to create your portable tiny house is the trailer frame. You can find plenty of used ones on Craigslist if you wish, otherwise they can be bought new, or even be custom built to meet your requirements. A metal shop can be the ideal place to ask if you want a custom frame built.

Many people like to have a complete plan ready before buying any materials, but if you are building a portable tiny home, that totally will depend on the size and specifications of your trailer. If you are looking to buy a trailer 2nd hand, you'll need to have a rough idea of your plan, but won't be able to create anything too specific until the trailer arrives.

Just like with a standard tiny house build, you do not want to buy every single thing 2nd hand. Electrical components, plumbing, and framing lumber are all things that it pays to buy new. If any of these materials are of poor quality, things can go seriously wrong!

The following is a basic order of operations for when building your portable tiny home.

Trailer

The trailer is the first part of your tiny home that you'll need. This is one area where it can pay to invest in a high quality, steel trailer of an adequate size. Make sure that the trailer is rust-proofed, and painted to ensure its longevity.

Floor & Frame

Once you have your trailer and have made a plan for your tiny house, it's onto the next stage. Here you will be putting together the flooring and the framework of the house. If you're not experienced at all with carpentry, it can really pay to hire a contractor to help you with this stage!

Make sure that you are using high quality lumber during this step. You will need to secure lumber to your trailer for your sub-floor, and create the entire frame, making space for doorways and windows. It's very important to have either drawn a plan up yourself, or hired somebody else to do so prior to beginning this stage. When framing for windows.

Sheathing

Once you've built the frame of your house, test-fit windows, raised the walls, squared and braced them, and secured your frame to your trailer using anchors, it's onto the next step: sheathing.

Here you need to measure and plan your panel layout, cut all pieces, and allow for approximately a 1/8" expansion gap between sheets of plywood.

Test-fit all sheathing before applying glue to all studs, tacking in place with nails, and screwing the panels together. Make sure that you are using screws that are designed for treated wood when doing this, or you'll damage your plywood! Also, don't forget to install your installation when raising the walls and creating the rough interior.

Windows & Doors Openings

Double check all of your window and door dimensions here, and leave a little extra room for expansion.

Cut out all of your window holes using a plunge router, and apply house wrap, Tyvek, or Typar. Cut your house wrap and test fit your windows.

If all fits, install your windows and shim, tack with a few screws and check it again for functionality. Make sure that your windows are secured as per the manufacturers specifications, and leave the bottom edge of the windows unsealed to allow for water drainage.

Roofing

In this stage, you need to first frame your roof. Depending on the type of roof you choose to use, steps will vary slightly.

Construct the trusses as per your plan, ensuring that the height of your house stays under the legal requirement of your state (usually 13.5 feet). If you want to add a skylight, build headers for the rough opening.

Once the framing of the roof is constructed, you'll need to add the roof sheathing. Cut your boards, glue the truss edges, use 'H' clips between sheets, and secure with nails and screws. If you have a skylight in your plan, you can now install it at this stage.

Door(s)

Here you will either build a door, or use a pre-purchased one. Test fit the door with your frame, shim, and secure it.

Siding

Now it is time to prepare the sides of your house. Tape house wrap seams, install furring strips, and paint both sides of the siding.

Once that's complete, you can hang the siding.

Trim Work

Now it's time to make your project look more like a house!

Here you can add fascia boards, and install a drip edge.

You can also finish the roofing now by applying an ice and water shield, installing a reflection barrier, and installing furring strips.

Plumbing & Electrical

Here you should plan out where you want drains, inlets, holes in floor, locations of outlets, fans, sockets, etc. You should however, leave the actually installation to professionals during this stage.

Follow your plans during this stage, making sure that all of your plumbing and electrical is accounted and planned for.

If needed, you can also make room for your gas lines at this point.

Insulation

Here we will be adding insulation throughout the house. Use foam in the edges, and install a vapor barrier of 6-millimeters in thickness. Ensure that all materials that come into contact with insulation foam are okay and do not react to it.

Install Major Appliances

Here you can install things such as a water heater, shower, and heater.

Flooring

Depending on your flooring type, this step will vary. Follow the manufacturers directions and lay your flooring, be it tiles, floorboards, or something else. Make sure that your flooring is trimmed around lights and edges. You may also need to install skirting boards depending on your design.

Walls

Hang your wall panels now, making sure to trim around lights and edges.

Finishing Touches

Now the majority of your home is built, it's time to add everything else! Here you'll need to have professionals install all of your plumbing, the toilet and shower, lights, an oven or stovetop, and any gas lines.

You can also build some interior framing here, such as cupboards and shelves, or you can fit pre-built ones. Install a bed frame, cupboards, and seating here.

Celebrate

Congratulations, you've just built a portable tiny house! It's time to test it out on the road!

Chapter 11:
How Long Will The Home Last?

Every single house, no matter the type, needs some maintenance over time if it is to remain intact. However, with tiny houses, the question of 'How long will my home last?' is often overlooked.

Tiny houses typically cost a lot less than a traditional home, and can be made of different materials than a normal build. These factors do play a role in the longevity of your home, and how long it will last before needing some extreme renovations!

What is Your Tiny House Built Out Of?

The materials you choose to build you house with play a massive role in its longevity.

Many people choose to use shipping containers for the fact that they are inexpensive and also sturdy. This building material however, can really affect how well your house ages. A massive factor is whether you chose to use new containers, or used ones.

A typical used shipping container is an average of 10 years old by the time you purchase it! This will obviously vary from place to place, but it's an important question to ask before making a purchasing decision. These containers are faced with extreme conditions, and even though that is what they are designed to withstand, it can take its toll!

Your average shipping container will last 20-25 years before needing any repairs, or being affected too heavily by the weather. But, if you take good care of it, have it painted, rust-proofed, insulated, and sealed, then it can often stay in great condition for much, much longer!

If you are using traditional building materials, your tiny house can be expected to last for longer, though it may cost more to build initially.

Portable tiny houses are a common exception though, and may require more maintenance than stationary homes. Due to their nature, these houses have a lot of moving parts such as wheels, portable plumbing systems, batteries, and intricate technology. With all of these small parts, the likelihood of something needing replacing is quite high.

If you plan to build a portable home, keep in mind that there will be ongoing maintenance costs to keep everything in working order. However, just like with a traditional home, if you take a preventative approach it will last quite well!

Preventative Measures

Taking preventative actions in maintaining your house will play a huge role in its longevity. Spending a little money and time each year to work on your house can save you a lot in the long-run!

Doing simple things like properly insulating your house, sealing any cracks, making sure your house is re-painted every few years, and rust-proofing your house periodically will play a huge role in how long your house stays in good condition.

External Cladding

Having external cladding on your home can greatly increase its longevity! This is particularly important if your house is made from a shipping container. Rather than having the bare container face the outside world, you may want to consider wooden panels, plaster, brick, render, or some other form of external cladding to protect against the elements.

Weather

The weather where you live can play a large role in the condition of your house, and also the amount of up-keep required.

If you live in an extremely hot environment, you will need to use a heavy duty paint, and re-paint your home periodically to keep it in good condition.

In a cold environment, having proper insulation is equally vital. Ensuring that all cracks and holes are sealed is very important as to avoid any leakages and rust within your home.

In climates with a wide variance of temperatures you will need to be most careful. This is also equally true for anyone with a portable home as you may take it through extremely varying climates! For these conditions you'll want to ensure that insulation is properly installed, the house is re-painted regularly, and also that everything is rust-proofed.

So... How Long Will It Last?!

Just like with a regular home, there is no exact answer to this question.

Building your house the correct way, paying particular attention to the climate you will be living in can help a lot when it comes to longevity. Likewise, regular maintenance is absolutely key to keeping your home in great condition.

If you can achieve both of those things, your house should last just as long (if not longer) than a regular house!

Chapter 12: Insulation

Insulating your tiny house is an absolutely crucial step in ensuring that your house stays in good condition for a long time, and also that it's comfortable to live in.

Depending on your climate, budget, and design, different insulation options will need to be considered.

There are 8 primary types of insulation that you will want to look at:

Denim/Cotton Insulation

This type of insulation is created from cotton mill waste, and low grade recycled cotton. This type of insulation is very environmentally friendly, is non-toxic, and has a great ASTM fire rating. It is great for DIYers, however it can weigh twice as much as other insulation types, and can be high in pesticides depending on the manufacturer.

Fiberglass Insulation

This insulation type is created by fusing sand and recycled glass together at high heat. It is readily available, cheap, and simple to install. However, it has a low R value, is highly flammable, and can grow mold if exposed to water.

Rock Wool

This type on insulation is formed by heating basalt rocks or steel-mill slag in a surface to an extremely high temperature. It is highly flame-resistant, is inexpensive, and generally does not require the installation of a moisture barrier. On the negative side, it can hold a large amount of water if there is a leak, and the fibers can be lodged in the lungs, eyes, and skin if you don't use protective gear during installation.

Extruded Polystyrene Insulation

Also known as blueboard, this insulation type is manufactured in both low-density and high-density versions. It is easy to source, lightweight, and is strong. However, it is flammable and produced toxic fumes when burned. Additionally, it's creation is not very green, and has a high global warming potential.

Expanded Polystyrene

Also referred to a beadboard, this insulation type is also manufactured in low and high density formulas. It is the least rigid foam, has less on a negative effect on the ozone, and is lightweight. It is however flammable, and while it doesn't lead to ozone depletion, its creation does produce a lot of smog.

Polyisocyanurate Foam Boards

Often referred to as polysio, this insulation is a high-density, rigid foam board. It has the highest R value per inch out of all the types of rigid foam boards, is lightweight, and resists moisture and air filtration. On the negative side, it is quite expensive, is flammable, and produces toxic gases when burned.

Open Cell Insulation

In this insulation system, the gas pockets connect with one another. A bath sponge is an example of how this insulation appears to look. They are very low in cost, and some brands use no ozone-depleting compounds. However, the health risks with this type of insulation are high, as all spray foams contain toxic ingredients.

Closed Cell Insulation

This type of insulation is much denser than open cell foam. It has one of the highest R ratings, and adds structural support to the house frame. As a spray foam however, it does contain toxic ingredients, such as isocyanate.

What to Consider

So, what should you consider when deciding upon which of the 8 insulation types above are best for you?

There are 3 main criteria you should consider when making your choice:

R Value

The R value represents the extent to which your insulation resists heat-flow. Essentially, the higher the R value, the more value your insulation has. This is particularly important if you will be building in a cold climate.

Loose Fill Vs. Closed

Insulations are either closed or they are loose fill. Closed insulations create a vapor barrier and will give you extra strength within your walls. An example of this is a spray foam.

Loose fill insulations require material to be loosely packed within you walls. This type of insulation can be easily installed, and fit well into awkward spaces.

Environmental Impact

As you saw, many insulations types are not environmentally friendly, and contribute to ozone depletion. When building your home, you get to choose if you'd like to use green materials during your construction. These can often be more expensive, but if you have the money to spend, are the best choice to make.

Chapter 13:
Minimalism

A book about tiny houses would not be complete without covering the topic of minimalism!

Minimalism is one of the great drivers behind the tiny house movement, and is taking the world by storm.

As commercialism runs rampant, some people in society are beginning to repel against this cultural shift, and move towards a more simplistic life with less material possessions. Doing this not only saves them a lot of money, but has been anecdotally reported to make most a lot happier!

What is Minimalism?

Minimalism is quite simply a lifestyle choice to possess less material items. A simple definition is: 'To live only with things that you really need'.

While some minimalists may also have a few material possessions that aren't absolutely vital, the idea is to live with less.

Most people have thousands of dollars of material possessions that they never use or even look at. We tend to accumulate these things over time, and they end up being nothing more than a burden; both physically and financially.

These unnecessary possessions can often stop people from living the life they desire. Be that to travel, or to simply have the freedom to spend money on experiences rather than things.

The tiny house movement is driven primarily by the minimalist lifestyle. People are starting to want more experiences, whilst having less 'stuff'. A tiny house saves people money, forces them to get rid of useless things that they don't need, and often times allows them to travel if their home is portable!

How to Embrace a Minimalist Lifestyle

From where you are now, it might seem like a massive and almost impossible step to take to embrace this style of living.

We can become overly attached to our possessions – even the ones we never use or even look at.

Things often have sentimental value also, making them that much harder to part with.

A great first step for testing this lifestyle is to create a stock list of sorts. Walk around your house, and compile a list of all of the things that you have. List all of the appliances, gadgets, furniture, books, movies, souvenirs, old presents, things hidden away in your garage, and everything else that you can find!

Next, go through your list and make a note of all of the items that you could live without, and/or rarely use.

You might be surprised at how much 'stuff' you've accumulated that doesn't really add anything to your life. You'd also be surprised at how much money you could make by listing a lot of these things on eBay – greatly helping to fund your tiny house build!

If you're ready to dive into the tiny house lifestyle, then it's time to get rid of these things! If you are struggling to get rid of them, but can't fit them into your new home, paying for storage somewhere is a great idea. Some things have sentimental value, and others can simply be difficult to part with after a long time of owning them. Put these things into storage, or give them to a friend or relative to look after. After a while without them, you might come to the realization that you don't 'need' these things after all, and will be ready to part ways with them altogether.

Chapter 14:
FAQs

When researching and building a tiny house, lots of questions will arise. Here are some of the most commonly asked questions, along with their answers.

Q: What is a tiny house?

A: A tiny house is a home built on a smaller scale. It is typically the size of an RV or a trailer, and is often mobile. Typically, their square footage does not pass 300 square feet, and they focus on making the most use of their small size.

Q: How much does a tiny house cost?

A: This can vary a lot, depending on a lot of factors. On the low-end, there are accounts of people building their own tiny houses using second hand materials for as little as $3000! However, the average DIY cost comes in at around $20,000 and for a professionally built home you can expect to pay double that.

Q: Can I finance a tiny home?

A: Because of their low price, financing a tiny house is uncommon. However, you may be able to secure financing as long as your build meets your local building standards and is approved by your bank or lending institution.

Q: Where can I buy a tiny house?

A: If you'd prefer to buy a tiny house rather than build one yourself, the best place to search is the internet. There may be tiny-house builders in your area, or people with portable tiny homes that are willing to have the tiny house transported to you.

Q: Where can I buy plans for a tiny house?

A: There are a huge number of websites selling tiny house plans. A great one to begin with is:

- http://www.tinyhousedesign.com/plans

Q: Where can I park or build my tiny house?

A: If your tiny house is portable and meets RV specifications and requirements, they can usually be parked at trailer parks, though you will need to check with the park beforehand. If you're building a tiny house, this depends totally upon your location. You will need to check with local government to ensure that your plan meets the local requirements, and is provided with a building permit.

Q: Are tiny houses legal?

A: If their build is approved by the government where you reside, then yes. Do keep in mind however that the tiny house movement is new, and is still quite a grey-area in many states, particularly for portable tiny houses.

Q: Do I need building permits for a tiny house?

A: Yes, just like with a regular house you will need to acquire the correct permits for your state.

Q: What kind of toilets and plumbing do people install in tiny houses?

A: In portable tiny houses, most people install composting toilets, such as the sawdust toilet. For stationary houses, conventional plumbing can be used.

Q: How do you heat and cool a tiny house?

A: To save space, most people use small propane or electric heaters for their tiny homes. For cooling, you can install a small air conditioner, and also use fans.

Q: How do you deal with grey water?

A: Waste water can be dealt with by installing a grey water system that can collect and dispose of the water. If your house is stationary, you can simply connect it to conventional plumbing.

Q: How much does a tiny house weigh?

A: Depending on your location, there are different size requirements to how much your tiny house is allowed to weigh. Typically tiny houses will vary from 16-foot up to 28-foot in length, and will weigh anywhere between 7,000lbs and 13,000lbs.

Q: What kind of trailer should I build my portable tiny house on?

A: This depends on your experience with working with metal. If you have experience doing metal work and welding, then a pre-used trailer may be suitable. Otherwise, it's recommended to buy a new trailer, or get one custom made to meet your specifications.

Q: How many people can live in a tiny house?

A: A full family can live in a tiny house, just like they would share an RV or caravan. This all depends upon your design, and number of beds you include in your tiny house.

Q: Are tiny houses off the grid?

A: They can be if you choose to install solar panels and make use of this energy. Typically however you will also need some back-up form of power as things such as air conditioners, heaters, and ovens can use a lot of juice!

Q: Can I insure my tiny house?

A: In some cases, yes. This is something you'll need to contact your insurance agent about, and will depend on a number of factors, including whether your tiny house is stationary or portable.

Chapter 15:
Tiny House Ideas

In this chapter there are a few images of some of the coolest tiny houses to help give you some inspiration for your very own tiny house!

If you'd also like to view some some complete tiny house plans, there are some free resources available that I would recommend. You can head to the following websites to download complete building plans, totally for free:

- https://www.thebalance.com/free-tiny-house-plans-1357142

- http://www.tinyhousedesign.com/free-plans/

- http://tinyhousetalk.com/plans/

Conclusion

Thanks again for taking the time to read this book!

You should now have a good understanding of tiny houses, and be ready to begin planning the build of your very own!

If you enjoyed this book, please take the time to leave me a review on Amazon. I appreciate your honest feedback, and it really helps me to continue producing high quality books.